FROM *My* EYES

How A Widowed, Uneducated, African-American Father Raised Eleven Children To Become Successful Adults

DORIS H. KOGO

iUniverse books may be ordered through booksellers or by contacting:

iUniverse
1663 Liberty Drive
Bloomington, IN 47403
www.iuniverse.com
844-349-9409

Because of the dynamic nature of the Internet, any web addresses or links contained in this book may have changed since publication and may no longer be valid. The views expressed in this work are solely those of the author and do not necessarily reflect the views of the publisher, and the publisher hereby disclaims any responsibility for them.

Any people depicted in stock imagery provided by Getty Images are models, and such images are being used for illustrative purposes only.
Certain stock imagery © Getty Images.

ISBN: 978-1-6632-5856-4 (sc)
ISBN: 978-1-6632-5857-1 (e)

Library of Congress Control Number: 2023922899

Print information available on the last page.

iUniverse rev. date: 03/15/2024

I gratefully acknowledge Bobette Atkins, S. R. and family members for their support and help.

Doris H. Kogo

Doris H. Grant

This is the story of how an African- American family of eleven children was raised by their father, through hardships, disadvantages, and tragedies under circumstances most people could not nor would not have wanted to endure. Yet those eleven became educated and productive individuals. This father showed by example, managed to keep a job, never used alcohol, cursed nor complained in front of his children.

THE BEGINNING

My father, **Douglas Grant Sr.** was born in **Shreveport, Caddo Parish, Louisiana on March 3, 1910.** He was average height, thin, weighing approximately 150 pounds with an infectious smile.

His parents were Ira and Victoria Faulkner Grant (daughter of John Faulkner).

He had seven siblings:

John, born in 1900, Coushatta
Lucille born 1902 Coushatta
J.P. born 1904, Coushatta
Nellie, born in 1906 Coushatta
Archie born in 1908, Coushatta
Annisteen, born 1912, Shreveport
James born 1917, Shreveport

His grandfather, James Grant I:

Was a Caucasian, born in 1835, in Coushatta. He married an African American woman, Alice Graham. She was born in 1850. They had seven sons:

Dewitt Clinton I, born Coushatta, 1875
James Grant, Jr. born Coushatta, 1876
Ira, born Coushatta, 1880
John W. born Coushatta, 1882
Abraham, born Coushatta, 1883
I.T., born 1885, Coushatta
Samuel Houston, Coushatta 1886

His great grandfather, Taylor Grant, born 1815 (Taylor could be surname) was a white slave owner:

He married a mulatto woman by the name of Sarah Brown, born 1815, in Halifax, Virginia. Sarah's father was a white slave owner by the name of Warner Brown. She could not read or write. Sarah and Taylor had the following children:

Martha, born 1831
Miranda, born 1833
Fletcher, born 1835
James, born 1835
Melissa, born 1836
Wesley, born 1839
Amelie, born 1843
Walter, born 1850

Douglas Grant Sr. 1943

James Grant I

Uncle J.P. Grant

Aunt Lucille Grant–Cato

Uncle John and Son

FLEEING LOUISIANA

The Grant family lived in Shreveport in rural areas and worked as sharecroppers and domestic workers. The children never had a formal education but could read and write. They, along with the adults, had to help in the fields and each other. A normal day was up early, draw water from the well, work in the fields until dark. Education was not encouraged nor a priority. They were raised not to ask questions or unset white people. Things such as smoking tobacco were a treat and the children would go into the open fields to smoke at an early age, my father being one of them. Food was always at a shortage for the family as well as clothing and supplies.

Grandmother Victoria became pregnant with Uncle James in 1917 and died in child birth. This was devastating to Grandfather Ira. He asked Victoria's sister, **Sallie** to please come and take care of baby James as well as the children. A year later, 1918, he married Hattie Cato, thus began the union of the Grant and Cato families.

Life became routine for the family working in the fields, **Aunt Sallie** helping with the care of the children and being supportive. A few years later, a white farmer appeared and accused a Grant family member of stealing one of his cows. The family denied it and carried on with their daily routine. One of the family members told Grandfather Ira the **Ku Klux Klan** was looking to get revenge on behalf of the farmer. This frightened Grandfather Ira so that in the middle of the night, the family fled to Oklahoma and lived with Native Americans.

They lived with the Indians for many years, dating Indian women. The family missed Louisiana and after many years, returned to Shreveport and continued as sharecroppers and domestic workers. Uncle John on the advice of William Cato Sr. returned to Oklahoma and meets his beautiful sister Lucille Grant. They soon married and stayed in Oklahoma.

My father was a hard worker and a good athlete. He was soon playing baseball for the **Negro League in Shreveport.** He often told us he could never hit a curve ball. While working in the fields he met my mother, **Nellie Mae Shields** born in Elysian Fields, Texas on July 24, 1922. He was struck by her beauty and maturity and her strong bond with her mother. Her mother, **Millie Broadnax Shields,** born with anisomelia, had two older daughters, Ellen Fields and Asalyn Carter. My parents married in January 1935.

Her mother, Millie Broadnax Shields a mullato, was a midwife and to my knowledge, she was a single woman though it was noted she was married to Henry Shields. As an adult, I went to Elysian Fields and spoke to Aunt Asalyn, and asked who my mother's real father was. She said, "His name is Elijah Mahon." I never forgot that. We have no information about him at all.

Aunt Sallie Dupree in 1971, Age 96

Nellie Grant and Archy

Grandma Millie Broadnax Shields and Her Cousin Johnnie

Great Grandfather Jordan Broadnax

THE GRANT CHILDREN

ARCHY GRANT – BORN IN MARSHALL, TEXAS NOVEMBER 1935

The first born and most admired by my parents, he had a fair complexion, and he was part of the reason they left the south. My father did not want him to become as my father would say, "just another cotton picker". Dee Dee, as we called him, was average height like my father, quiet, and serious about school, sports, and his appearance. He did not interact with the younger siblings and was aloof. He was considered to be more intelligent than most kids in the neighborhood and more reliable. He got a paper route as a teenager and was thought to be the most reliable paperboy they ever had. He never missed doing his route, and his customers never missed receiving their paper. He was articulate, mild mannered, mature, and thoughtful. He, like most kids in the neighborhood, played sports, formed a neighborhood singing group and was gone most of the evening until dark. If there wasn't any dinner left, he just didn't eat anything.

DOUGLAS JR. BORN JANUARY 1937

Douglas, nicknamed Niche, was premature, born at 7 months. The nurse said he was so small she called him tee niche. That name stuck with him his entire life. He could not pronounce Archy's name and would call him Dee Dee. To this day we call him Dee Dee. We often called him the Mexican due to his complexion, his short stature and curly hair. He spoke softly as did both of my parents. He was a sportsman and was seldom home, more so than Archy. He was a practical joker, at times mean and generous. He loved being with his friends and was often grumpy.

He was my parent's most challenging son. I suppose because he was hardheaded. I recall the police beat him up, and my father went to the police station to complain.

CHARLES, BORN JULY 1938

Was nicknamed Peter, but I never knew why. He looked more like my mother and her relatives than any of my other brothers did. He was tall, lanky and had light skin. Charles adored my mother dearly and she him.

He never complained about the fact that he had to sleep on the back porch. He loved playing many sports, including football, basketball, and ran track. All the teenagers spent time together at what we called The Wreck. It was a community center that held basketball tournaments and games, girl scouts, ping pong, track and had meeting rooms. We loved being there, and we always knew we could find our siblings and friends there.

My brothers seldom did chores. We each were supposed to have a turn washing the dishes. Charles would pay one of us to wash dishes for him. One thing none of us could get out of was going to church. If we didn't attend, then we could not go to the movies.

VIRGINIA, BORN DECEMBER 1939

Virginia resembled my father more than any of us. She was beautiful, gentle like a lamb, thin and emotional. The girls shared one bedroom as did the boys. Our home had three bedrooms. My parents were in one, the girls were in another, and the boys and Charles slept on the enclosed porch. Someone always wet the bed. It could be chaotic in the mornings with my mother always up early to get us up, fix breakfast, iron someone's clothes, and comb our hair. We always had cereal or grits for breakfast. Occasionally, she made pancakes and her own syrup to go with them.

ALMA, BORN MARCH 1941

Alma Marie, as my father often called her, was very fair, had long black hair, and the boys loved her. She was outgoing, loved to look nice, and was a good housekeeper. When my mother got a job as a housekeeper, Virginia and Alma were in charge of cleaning the house. Virginia and Alma sang in the youth choir at Union Baptist Church. The entire complex attended that small white church. Alma and Virginia loved to sing as did my mother. I remember my mother had a beautiful voice. However, my mother was very shy, and she never sang in the church choir as several of the other mothers in Chabot did.

Alma always seemed to have a boyfriend or boys were interested in her. She loved school as did Virginia. The two always seemed to be carrying books and wore scarves around their necks.

HOWARD, BORN NOVEMBER 1942

Howard resembled both parents. My father always said, "He looks just like his momma." Howard was thin, tall for his age, seemed to know all the kids in the neighborhood and adored my mother. He was always in a fight and many times my mother had to talk to him about fighting. He was an excellent rock thrower. We always said he threw curve rocks and never missed his mark. Neighbors complained to my parents that my brothers were throwing rocks and breaking their windows. Howard was left-handed and was the best rock thrower. Howard was close to my cousin Ronnie who was the same age. Ronnie's mother, Levator, was my first cousin who came to California with her father, Uncle J.P. At one time she stayed with us and always took Ronnie everywhere she went.

Ronnie had an unstable childhood. Levator was a good person and friendly, but at times she could not control her drinking and was known to get into fights at bars and landed in jail. We never met Ronnie's father, and I never knew his name. Unlike the rest of us, Ronnie was born in Oklahoma. When Levator was in jail, Ronnie lived with Aunt Nellie. She spoiled him terribly, and eventually she and her husband, Isadore Andrews, adopted him. Ronnie had a half-sister, Vicky, who is named after my grandmother. Vicky stayed with Levator most of the time, but we would see her at Aunt Nellie's during the summer. Vicky would occasionally stay with us in Vallejo.

Cousin Ronnie Andrews

Isadore and Nellie Grant Andrews

THE MOVE TO CALIFORNIA

During that time, the United States became involved in WWII. My father and Uncle J.P. heard the military was hiring workers for the various shipyards. He travelled by train to California bringing my three oldest brothers with him, and leaving my mother in Shreveport with Howard, Virginia and Alma. He returned to Louisiana and told my mother there were jobs and places to stay called projects in Vallejo. The entire family travelled to California by train, with my father's brothers following with their families, Uncle J.P. (John Pierpont), Uncle Archy, Aunt Ellen Writt (my mother's sister with her three children and husband) followed along with Aunt Nellie (my father's sister). We all lived in the same housing development, Chabot Terrace in Vallejo, and in the same house until each found their own place and employment at Mare Island.

Uncle James his wife and two children: James Ray (James Ray's twin sister Johnnie Fay died at one month old) and Betty Jean (whose real name was Victoria, also named after my grandmother) soon joined us in California. The marriage did not last and he married his second wife a wonder woman by the name of Bertie Mae. James Ray and Betty lived in San Francisco with their mother. Aunt Bertie Mae was a loving, happy woman and an excellent housekeeper and cook. She was unable to have children of her own and we, in a sense, became her family and children. She was my mother's best friend and companion.

The move was good for us. My father got a job working at Mare Island. For extra money most of my relatives got part time work picking fruit in the fields of the Suisun Valley in Fairfield.

I remember going along with my brothers, sisters, Uncle J.P to help early in the morning. My brothers continued to pick fruit in the summer months via jobs Uncle J.P. got them. I can still hear the truck pulling up in front of our house blowing the horn for them at 5am in the morning. My brother Archy was the only brother that was not asked to pick fruit as my parents had higher hopes for him to do something with his life. He is also the only sibling I can remember that never got a whipping.

CAROLYN, BORN OCTOBER 1944

My mother was pregnant with Carolyn when they moved to California. Because my mother wanted to be close to her mother, she returned to Shreveport to have Carolyn. Carolyn was the thinnest of us all. She was, light-skinned, and the boys said she was cute but too shy. She was emotional, seemed to do her own thing and forbid anyone to touch her things, e.g., comb, shoes, etc. Often, we had to wear each other clothes, and Carolyn did not like sharing. Carolyn would report us to my parents if we used or touched anything that belonged to her. She liked school and neighborhood friends.

DORIS H. BORN DECEMBER 1945

My mother became pregnant with me and again wanted to return to Louisiana to have me. My father said no, we are not returning, I was born in Vallejo, California. I Doris Helen, as relatives always called me, was number eight of what was to become eleven children. Aunt Ellen wanted to name me Helen, my mother preferred Doris. The first memory I recall was in 1947, I was sitting in a highchair in the kitchen with a picture of a bear on a lid. My parents, Douglas and Nellie Shields Grant, (Tet, as my relatives called her) were looking at me with admiration. My mother read in the papers there was to be a baby contest for my age group, the winner being crowned queen and king. Because the judges were white, she felt I did not have a chance. Aunt Ellen and Aunt Bertie Mae convinced my mother to enter me in the contest anyway. The winners were to be crowned baby queen and baby king. I won as baby queen. I remember all these strange people surrounding me and looking at me and congratulating my mother. She seemed nervous and a little worried. I do not know why I sensed that at the age of two. Looking back on it, I could only surmise why.

Aunt Ellen soon became a divorced woman. My cousin Winnie was dating a man by the name of Allen Davis. He was a frequent visitor to their home yet seemed to be more attracted to Aunt Ellen. After a period of time Davis and Aunt Ellen began dating and married. He was a cook in the Air Force and she later began travelling with him.

JEANETTE, BORN DECEMBER 1946

Jeanette and I are twelve months apart. She was born in Fairfield at the county hospital. She was the fairest of all the siblings. My Aunt Ellen and my cousin Winnie took me and cared for me because my mother just had Jeanette. I don't know how long I was under their care. I remember as a toddler seeing my mother hold a baby. We used to call Jeanette the white girl because she was so light and had light-brown hair. My Uncle James always called her dirty red because she had curly reddish hair. She adored my mother and my mother adored her. She was smart, always followed rules, was never in trouble, loved school and pleasing my mother. She was thin and short in stature like my mother. We were close, always played together, and people thought we were twins, not because we looked alike but because we were so close in age. Oftentimes my mother would dress us alike.

Jeanette was a good student and excelled in school. She was awarded a certificate in the fifth grade as captain of the crossing guards, and she still has it to this day.

LARRY, BORN AUGUST 1948

According to my cousin Winnie, Larry was born on the stretcher in Vallejo. My mother waited as long as she could before going to the hospital. The hospital would not admit her because of a past due bill.

Larry was a funny kid and always wanted to stay close to my mother and worshipped my father. Larry was his shadow. He loved playing cops and robbers and wanted to grow up to be a soldier or a cowboy. He was in the boy scouts, was a good ballplayer and played on our area little league team. We all attended his baseball games at Wilson Park. My father never missed a game, and we were proud to watch Larry play.

Daddy was as huge a Dodger fan as we are today. He loved most sports, football, basketball, etc. Jackie Robinson was his favorite player. He also admired Willie Mays.

We had a full basement underneath our home. The kids often played there, and we kept our pet chickens under the house for safe keeping from the cats in the neighborhood.

As a kid he had a paper route, got up early every morning before dark to deliver papers, and he still went to school.

MICHAEL, BORN SEPTEMBER 1953

It had been five years since we had had a baby in the house. When my mother became pregnant with Michael, Aunt Bertie Mae said they were all surprised because the doctor said she shouldn't have any more babies. We couldn't keep our hands off him. He was so cute, had curly hair, and my mother's complexion, and Aunt Bertie Mae loved him so. We couldn't wait to hold him after his morning bath. I noticed there were times when my mother would care for him and seemed at times sad.

At times she continued to dote on me. One Sunday evening, I was dressed in one of my Sunday dresses. My mother said, "Doris go outside and take a picture." She said it in a mean voice. I didn't want to stop playing and was annoyed. I took the camera and twisted a knob on the camera. I stood outside on a small hill while my mother took the picture. When it was developed, the picture was a double exposure. My mother looked right at me as if to say, "I know you did something". I didn't look at her. To this day, I cherish that picture because my mother had given me positive attention, and in our home, it was rare to get any attention at all.

Aunt Bertie with Michael

Michael Age 17 months

My father was working at Mare Island, and we always knew when he was expected home. I judged that by the time my mother would start cooking dinner. I would sit in the window, looking for him and listening for the sound of his car. When he walked in the door, we were so happy, fighting over who would get his house shoes as he was always tired. Larry would beat all of us to his house shoes.

There was no such thing as a formal lunch time in our house. We did not want to stop playing to eat lunch. If we became hungry, we would go inside and fix a sugar, syrup or butter sandwich with white bread. Dinner would mostly be beans and rice or spaghetti with no meat. Sundays were the only day we had meat.

My favorite food was candy. The corner grocery store was called the Little Store where we would purchase candy with money given to us by Uncle Archy. We purchased as much candy as we could get in the brown paper bag. My favorite was a Hollywood candy bar, winner sucker, because if you got a prize you got a second sucker for free, candy cigarettes, gum, jaw breakers and Kool-Aid.

If we didn't have any money, Jeanette and I would steal candy. We put our plan in place, went to the Little Store and stole candy. Unbeknownst to us, my brother Dee Dee was in the store and saw us. He told my mother, and she took out a ruler, made us hold out our hands and wacked each hand twice. It was so painful. Later my brother Dee Dee asked my mother what she did to punish us, and she told him what she had done. He talked to her regarding how she should punish us without whipping. Later, my mother went to the butcher to buy meat. She bought frankfurters to put in our spaghetti. While she was talking on the phone, Jeanette and I ate all the frankfurters. When she found out, she said "I know what I will do." She bought more frankfurters and fixed the spaghetti, but Jeanette and I had to eat our spaghetti without meat. I asked several times if we could have meat and she said no. We never did that again. From that lesson I learned how to think about a form of punishment without always hitting.

We had a mailman in the neighborhood who would get drunk every Friday after getting paid. The young boys in the neighborhood knew this and would, as they said, "roll him for his money" to supplement their income. All of them seemed to always have great looking hamburgers on the weekends.

Larry's 4th Birthday, Patricia and Diane Jackson, Jeannette Grant

Larry, Doris, Patricia Jackson, Cousin Vicki, Jeanette

Doris, Alma, and Carolyn

Doris Age 9

Alma went to the fair and won three baby chicks. They were so cute we kept them in the kitchen near the furnace for warmth and fed them all night. The following morning, we found one of them dead. I asked my mother what happened. She said, "I don't know it just died." We kept the two other chickens until they reached adulthood. At night we kept them under the house which was a full enclosed basement to keep the feral cats from eating them. In the morning we would let them roam around the yard. We had many feral cats in the neighborhood. On occasion the police would ask the residents which cats belonged to whom. If they were feral, the police would send out notices they would be shot on certain days. We had to stay indoors when this happened. Before they were shot, one of them killed one of the two remaining chickens. We were down to one chicken we called Brownie and our dog Trixie.

THE YEAR 1954

I was eight years old and in the third grade at Olympic School. I didn't like my hair in braids and would take them out after I got to school. My mother would scold me about it. We were given free lunch because my father never made enough money to support all of us. Our favorite lunch day was Friday because we had Sloppy Joes. I loved my mother's cooking, I especially liked spinach. Most of the kids hated it. I would eat theirs with delight. I was happy and healthy. I was called "the fat girl" by my relatives because Carolyn and Jeanette were so skinny. When I look back, I was just healthy. Jeanette was very picky. My mother was picky in that she didn't drink regular milk and certain foods she didn't like. I remember my mother ironing my dress in the dark and combing my hair. She was excited and reached down to hug me. The only time I remember her hugging me. My favorite teacher was Mrs. Dorothy Johnson, my third-grade teacher. I loved walking to school with friends some of whom I still have today. Mrs. Johnson was young, slim and always wore her hair in a bun. Occasionally, after school she would let us brush her hair and erase the blackboard. She was the first teacher that taught us about American Indians. On many days we had to duck under our desk for drill alarms as we thought at that time the Japanese would drop bombs on us.

When my mother came for a conference, Mrs. Johnson told her how well liked I was, but she felt I needed more attention at home. I recall my mother calling Aunt Bertie Mae telling her that, but she never said it to me. She seemed to not talk to me but to other people about me.

We did not have a television set, but we loved listening to programs on the radio. Every Sunday after church, we would sit on the floor in front of the radio and listen to the soap operas, *The Shadow, Boston Blacky, Amos and Andy, The Lone Ranger,* and boxing matches, Floyd Patterson, Sugar Ray Robinson, Jake Lamotta, etc. On certain days we could actually pick up the signal for the Dodgers game.

The only neighbors that had a television set were the Dunns'. All the kids in the neighborhood would go their house and watch *Howdy Doody, Brother Buzz, Brer Rabbit, Little Lulu,* and *Popeye the Sailorman.* Eventually we got a television, and my mother would watch the soup operas. I loved watching them with her. Our favorites were "Love of Life" and "Search for Tomorrow". It seemed like every single day, Mother would wash clothes on a wash board. We finally got a washing machine and she continued to dry clothes on a wire clothesline in the backyard that we shared with our next door neighbor.

Postcard to Mother from Aunt Ellen 1954

THE HANGING

We didn't have a telephone for a very long time. Across the street on Pike Street was a telephone booth. All the kids used that as a home number. That phone was always ringing. I remember Dee Dee running over there to answer the phone. The girls would use our neighbor, the Jackson's, phone because Virginia had become their babysitter.

One evening, one of the Jackson children came over and told Virginia she had a phone call. I loved going over their home to play with their children. Virginia was rushing down the back stairs to answer the phone and I said, "I want to go," She said, "No." I continued to follow her down the stairs with Virginia looking back and running at the same time. Our next-door neighbor who shared the outdoor wire clothesline with us was hanging clothes. Suddenly, Virginia was hanging in the wire clothesline, it broke, and she was lying on the ground unconscious. I went up to her, not knowing what was wrong, looking down in wonder. Our neighbor started screaming and putting wet clothes on her face saying, "Oh Lord help. Mrs. Grant, Mrs. Grant." She ran up the backstairs into our house. The next thing I remember is the fire department arriving, carrying Virginia into the house, and laying her on the sofa. My mother was sitting in a chair next to her crying. I watched it all from across the room. My father arrived home while the firemen continued to work on her. I don't know how much time passed, but Virginia threw up, "Something as green as grass" as my mother described it. The fireman asked Virginia if she knew her name, where she was etc. They figured out she would be all right. The fireman said if not for the clothesline breaking, she would have died from hanging. After that, we got a phone.

HALLOWEEN

We all loved the coming holidays starting with Halloween. None of the neighborhood children had costumes, but we didn't care. All the neighbors would always have plenty of candy, homemade cupcakes, and popcorn balls. Before we went trick or treating, my mother would tell the older kids who was responsible for whom. We would leave home with brown paper bags or pillowcases. Upon returning home, we would empty our bags on the floor, and we would all go through them laughing and exchanging candy. My mother loved it as she would eat as much candy as we did.

CHRISTMAS HOLIDAYS AT SCHOOL AND HOME

It was an exciting, joyous time. I loved the holidays. Our third grade was scheduled to sing Christmas carols on the school stage. It was time for our class to enter the stage and sang. My white classmates were placed in the front row and the minorities were placed in the back row. The unwritten school policy was that all African American students were to be placed in the back. Mrs. Johnson did not seem to like the policy but did as she had to do. My mother and father came, and I was so proud.

During Christmas Holidays we exchanged gifts at school. I received a small, comb and brush set. Walking home from school, I dropped the gift and turned around to go back and find it. It was gone. I was afraid to let my mother know I had been careless. When I walked in the door, I wouldn't look at her. My mother gave me a look that only a mother could as though she knew. Later that evening, she called Aunt Bertie Mae and said, "Doris lost her gift." I didn't say a word. It was never mentioned again.

The excitement in the air at this time of year was the happiest time of my life. My mother went shopping with Aunt Bertie Mae and came home with so much food for the holidays and a Christmas tree. Our Christmas tree had so many lights we couldn't keep our hands off it. The bubble light was my favorite. My mother started cooking Christmas dinner, stuffing the turkey, making pies and cakes, rolls, cranberry sauce, etc. She always let us lick the spoon and bowl after making a cake. We received dolls and clothes for Christmas. My mother would occasionally make our clothes, but they were mostly made by Aunt Nellie. On that day we were allowed to enter my parent's bedroom and show them our gifts. We played outside with all the many kids in the neighborhood. Most of the families had a large number of children. The only couple I knew who had just one child was the next door neighbors, and we called him Donny boy. We all knew our prayers except for him. He would come over and ask us to teach him the Lord's Prayer because he feared getting a whipping for not knowing it.

Uncle James would pile us in the car with Aunt Bertie Mae and my mother in the front seat. We would drive around looking at all the Christmas decorations. Santa Claus and singers would come to our neighborhood and sing Christmas songs and give out candy. I was so fascinated with Santa I would follow him for blocks in the dark until I knew the dividing line to return home. As an older child, I was almost in shock to learn there was no Santa Claus.

During the holidays, my mother and I would walk to Uncle James and Aunt Bertie Mae's. I remember we left for home walking after dark. I was afraid of the dark and held on tightly to her. Two white men approached us and asked my mother if she wanted a ride. She calmly said, "No thank you". I was so frightened of them; I couldn't wait to get home. I learned from that experience what to say when a stranger approaches and how to stay calm.

A few days later, Aunt Bertie Mae asked if I could spend the night. My mother said yes which made me very happy. During the entire day and night at their home they argued constantly which was a shock to me because I never heard them speak to each other that way. The following day, which was Sunday morning, they continued to argue over who was going to fix my breakfast. Uncle James said, "She is my niece not yours; I will fix her breakfast". Aunt Bertie Mae said, "She doesn't like her eggs that way". It went on and on. Finally, I told Aunt Bertie that I was leaving for home. She said all right. I left without breakfast. When I returned home, I told my mother of the argument. She didn't seem surprised.

WHY? JANUARY, 1955

It was just after my 9th birthday. The weather was cold as I walked to school with my friends. We loved the sound of the crackling autumn leaves under our feet. We made sure we stepped on as many as we could. Everything was so routine in the house, my brothers were never at home, playing sports and their friends would come over to the house to pick them up to go outside and play, singing doo wop songs on the corner and talking to girls. Our sidewalk was being repaved, and we were told by the repair men not to walk on it.

Archy along with his neighborhood boys didn't walk on it, they just wrote their names all over it. Archy wrote his name and address. The following day, the police knocked on the door. They spoke to my mother and told her what Archy had done. They told her that the next time my parents would have to pay for the damage. My mother told my father when he returned home from work. To this day, I have never seen my father so angry.

We never used alarm clocks or had anyone to tell us to get up. The noise in the house, the fighting over the bathroom, the lights on in the bedroom, and the sound of my mother's voice was all the alarm we needed to get up.

The morning of Friday January 7 after the big kids left for school, I got dressed and noticed my mother was not up. I knocked on her bedroom door and asked her if she would comb my hair? She slowly got up, using the wall for support. I looked at her with a puzzled look on my face. She never needed help getting up. I sat on the floor in the living room waiting for her to sit behind me with comb and hair oil in hand. She touched my hair trying to part it, but her hands hardly moved, and I could not feel her securely braiding my hair. She took a long time, putting in loose braids which I never had.

Something was wrong. I turned and looked at her. She looked at me with tears in her eyes. I stared at her wondering what was wrong. She didn't say a word; I got up and went to school.

When I returned home, she was in bed. Aunt Bertie Mae, along with my cousin, Winnie, came over and each had a concerned look on her face. I heard my mother say, "If only I could just get up and do something, then I won't feel so tired." My aunt said, "No you stay in bed."

The weekend she lay in bed. My father and Aunt Bertie Mae were by her side and my cousin Winnie. On Monday, January 10, I got up, combed my hair as best I could and off to school.

I walked home with friends, stepping on every leaf, putting the events of the past days out of my mind. My mother was in bed and was talking softly. She looked different. I could not see her eyes; there were dark circles around her eyes. My brothers and sisters, Aunt Bertie Mae, our neighbor and Daddy were all crowded around her bed. She looked weak. My father called the doctor. He arrived and listened to her heart. I didn't hear what he said but everyone helped her get out of bed, she got dressed and she was taken to the hospital. She said to us, "Don't worry, I will be back."

Tuesday, January 11, I got up, combed my hair as best I could and went to school. I walked to school with my friends, always hurrying but making sure we didn't miss stepping on dry leaves. After school, I walked home again, not thinking about the events of the evening before.

I arrived at our home which was the middle of three apartments. I opened the door, and it was like a scene from the Wizard of Oz. The entire living room was filled with people, Aunt Bertie Mae, Winnie, Geneva, my cousin's wife, the next-door neighbor. Virginia was lying on the sofa screaming and crying. Aunt Bertie Mae was trying to comfort her, but she would not be comforted. I saw an empty chair by the door and sat in it staring at everyone. Winnie, with her green eyes, looked at me with a sorrowful look on her face, not saying a word. Just then Virginia held her head up and screamed, "Doris she is dead!"

I didn't know what to say as I didn't know what she meant. I had no reaction. I don't know how long I sat there, watching everyone scurry around, Geneva cooking, Aunt Bertie Mae trying to comfort Virginia with towels, fans, nothing worked. Virginia then passed out; several people were putting wet towels on her. Carolyn hid behind the refrigerator and refused to come out until my mother came home.

Cousin Winnie

My father's relatives arrived, and they were talking to my father who seemed to be in shock. I heard him say, "What am I going to do?" The next-door neighbor took me and Jeanette to her home to feed us. I don't have any memory of whether we ate.

Two days later there was a knock on the door. My father said, "Doris your teacher is here. It was Mrs. Johnson. She bent down to talk to me with a sad look and tears in her eyes. She hugged me and said, "Doris I am so sorry. Is there anything I can do?" I said no. I loved Mrs. Johnson. My father then said, "Doris I want you and Jeanette to go to my Cousin Babe's (Mary) house in Alameda." We didn't want to go because we did not know her, but we went without saying a word.

Babe lived in the projects in Alameda; most of housing in Alameda was projects. We slept in bunk beds in the bedroom where our cousin Wilburt, we called Brother, slept. I liked Babe right away and trusted her. I never in my life had asked adult questions; we only did as we were told, without question. I asked her, "What does it mean to die and what is a funeral?"

She told me everything and what happens after the funeral. To this day, I love Babe and I thought she was the wisest person I ever met.

THE FUNERAL

We stayed with Babe until the day of the funeral. We arrived home wearing a white dress and coat and white shoes. I have no memory of getting dressed and who dressed me. We pulled up in front of the house and someone carried me out of the car into the house. I was embarrassed, as I was not used to being carried. Babe and her husband took us to the church early. I remember her saying, "They have already arrived with the body." My mother was now just called a body. We did not see Wilburt again for over 25 years.

The ground was wet and muddy as it had rained for several days prior. We sat in the church waiting for everyone to arrive. One by one my brothers and sisters arrived. Aunt Bertie Mae sat with Virginia who was still in shock and crying uncontrollably. I watched everyone's reaction. My father was calm, sad, his brothers around him. My cousins Winnie, Betty and my mother's sister, Aunt Ellen, could not be comforted. She arrived from Germany with her husband and kept saying, "If only she would say something to me."

It was my turn to approach the casket and look at my mother. I remember a tortoise blue Chinese style blouse. She looked at peace. Larry said he touched her, and she was cold. Betty had to be carried out; Winnie's eyes were full of tears. We arrived at the cemetery walking up a muddy hill, my white shoes so caked in mud that it was an effort to lift my feet. The casket bearers, including my Uncle James, placed white gloves on the casket.

We all drove to our home where our relatives and neighbors were talking to my father, who seemed overwhelmed. The conversation was what to do with us and who was willing to take whom. My father couldn't talk or make a decision. He then talked to the oldest boy, Dee Dee, who said, and my father agreed, "We are staying together, including Michael, who was not quite two years old.

A wreath had been placed on our front door. I always hated that wreath. It seemed to stay on our door forever, as it was a sign that someone had died. A large meal had been prepared to serve a vast number of people in our home who came with gifts, money and clothes. After the large meal had been eaten, everyone departed. I returned to school after a two-week absence.

My father never spoke again about anything related to my mother or her illness. We still didn't know why she had died. I later learned from Virginia and my cousin Winnie that she was a diabetic and was using saccharin as a sugar substitute. She developed kidney problems and as a result died from complications of kidney failure due to diabetes.

Virginia and Alma took responsibility for us along with Aunt Bertie Mae and Winnie who were frequent visitors to our home. We were called "the little kids". We never received counseling as in those days you didn't discuss family affairs with strangers. Pastor Morris came to our home to speak to Daddy. After my mother's death, Daddy joined Union Baptist Church and became a deacon.

VALENTINE'S DAY, 1955

At that time the children exchanged Valentine cards with each other by giving our cards to the teacher and she called each child's name to come up and get their cards. My name was called so often I never got a chance to sit down. I was so grateful and happy. Our lives went on with the routine of Virginia and Alma getting us up and ready for school, breakfast and out of the house.

SUMMER VACATION, 1955

School is out for the summer! As always, we went to Stockton to stay with Aunt Nellie and our cousin Ronnie. She had an enclosed back porch, three bedrooms and a garage converted into living quarters for the handyman, Pork Chop. We all called him Porky. He took care of the grounds and did handy work for my aunt and uncle. He drank constantly but was not inebriated. He was also an intellectual. He would often tell us not to play behind the running car as the fumes, carbon monoxide, were poison. Aunt Nellie was the housekeeper for a well-to-do family in Stockton by the name Greer. Mr. Greer owned a large, successful auto business called Greer's Autos. They adored Aunt Nellie, with her big wide warming smile, cute face and straight black hair. She was the most energetic woman I have ever known. She never stopped moving. We would accompany her to the golf course to bring Uncle Issy a home cooked lunch, as he maintained the greens there. It was always so hot in Stockton; I didn't like the weather. We spent our days at the park, the park pool and attending the state fair. Aunt Nellie used to bet on the horses and give us her winnings to get into the fair. We always went to the fair at night as it was too hot during the day. Our instructions were to meet her in the front at the end of the fair by a certain time. We loved it. Aunt Nellie knew a baker who would give her dozens donuts early in the morning. We would go with her to pick them up. She was always nervous about blowing the car horn so early in the morning, fearing she would wake up the neighborhood. We loved our donuts and milk breakfast, something we would not get at home.

Vicky would join us in Stockton and on occasion and stay with us in Vallejo. She lived with her mother, Levator, most of the time. We thought of Vicky as our sister. Aunt Nellie had a son, Booker T. Kado who lived in Los Angeles. He was one of the most handsome men I have ever seen. We seldom saw him and wondered why his last name was spelled Kado instead of Cato as was the spelling of our other Cato cousins.

As adults we were told that Aunt Nellie went to Oklahoma to help my Aunt Lucille Cato and Uncle William Cato Sr. with the birth of one of her children. She became pregnant by William Cato Sr.; the circumstances are still a question. Some say she was raped, others are not saying. The Cato children never knew about Booker T until after William Cato's death, they found letters to and from Booker T, via a girlfriend.

We all slept in the same bed at Aunt Nellie's. She would wash and press our hair during the day but after trying to sleep in a hot room with no air conditioning or fan we sweat in our hair at night, so it never looked as though she did it. At night, Mr. Issy would come into our room at night with a flashlight shining it on us. I was afraid of him as he would put the light on each of our faces. I pretended to be asleep. Years later, Virginia and Alma told me he was displaying the same behavior towards them. They no longer would go to Stockton in the summer. They never told my father. Daddy let cousin Lawrence move in for a year. Lawrence sent money to Florence who moved to Aunt Nellie's. Their brother Wesley was now divorced. He had twins a boy and girl with his first wife, remarried and had another set of twins a boy and a girl. Once I was passing by the Aunt Nellie's bedroom door when I heard her say to him. "I saw you being nasty with that woman." Of course, he denied it.

On the flip side of him, he would purchase athletic shoes for my brothers and would always be the one to pick us up at night and drove us to Stockton. My father would join us on the weekends.

Booker T. Kado and Slick at Aunt Nellie's

Florence Cato, Doris Grant, Lawrence Cato

Virginia and Alma Grant

THE MOVE

We returned to our home after a long, hot summer in Stockton. Aunt Sallie stayed with us during the summer, helping Daddy with us and cooking. Our friends were talking about moving away. We were so sad to hear that. One by one families started to move away, and we didn't know why. We loved living there. Our church, school, family and friends all lived there or in another project called Floyd Terrace. Our neighbors on the right and left were still there. Donny boy told us he would be moving away as well. August 1955, my father said we are moving. We didn't know where or when. He asked us if we wanted to move to Floyd Terrace and we said no. After that he did not ask us any questions and we did not ask. We packed up all of our belongings, with Brownie the chicken but could not find Trixie. We arrived in South Vallejo to a huge, red stucco house on a hill. I got out of the car and looked straight up at the largest house I had ever seen. It was a Victorian house with six bedrooms, two downstairs and four upstairs one bathroom downs stairs and one upstairs with a spiral staircase, living room, dining room, kitchen and an enclosed back porch. We loved how roomy it was. We had a cherry and walnut tree in the backyard and a large area on the right side for growing a garden. My father quickly made a nice large garden.

The boys, Jeanette, Carolyn, and I slept upstairs. Downstairs my father's room was off the kitchen where Michael slept with him. Virginia and Alma slept in the bedroom off the dining room. We had one wall heater for the entire house that was in the dining room, and which proved to be challenging in the winter. We quickly made friends with another large family the Wells' that lived at the bottom of the hill.

At night, the house seemed spooky and dark. Michael was afraid of the dark and would not go upstairs. One of the bedroom upstairs was unoccupied as it had a door inside the bedroom that led to nowhere. If you opened the door you would fall to the ground.

Dee Dee drove back to Chabot to look for Trixie who had been his pet since childhood. He found him, and I never saw a dog so happy to see anyone.

THE KIDNAPPING

We settled in the house, exploring the neighborhood scouting for other children. I was nine and a half years old. The neighborhood was a conglomeration of whites, Chinese, Hispanics, Filipinos and a few African Americans. We loved the neighborhood and quickly made friends with another large family by the name of Wells that lived at the bottom of the hill. Daddy was now working at Napa State Hospital. We found the school we would be attending, Grant School, which was within walking distance. Late summer, my father said, "Doris the ex-neighbors children want you to go on a trip with them. I was excited to go with them and said yes. He said they will pick you up tomorrow evening. That evening, I waited at the dining room table with my father for the family to arrive. He opened the door and in came our ex-neighbors. I immediately became afraid, as he looked at me with a look I remembered in Chabot. My father was suspicious but did not say anything.

I got in the car with him in the front seat staying close to the passenger's door and looking at him. He started driving away and almost at once, he started asking me if I wanted anything, candy, a bike, and I said, "No". Now I was becoming nervous. He pulled up to a bike store and said look at the nice bikes. He started driving around looking out of the window towards the area where we used to live that was now just empty fields. I said, "I want to go home, take me home." He pulled over under a tree and pulled me over to him grabbing my dress. I pulled away; he pulled me back reaching under my dress. I started thinking about what to do to keep him from killing me. I thought about what I had learned in school during Mrs. Johnson's class. If ever kidnapped, try to grab the car keys, jump out of the car and run.

He pulled me over again; I grabbed the car keys from the ignition, opened the door and started running as fast as I could all the while crying looking around for the fastest way to get to a main street. I ran to a corner street and looked up. A car pulled up alongside of me with a Black couple inside. The man was driving and a woman in the front passenger seat. She rolled the window down and said to me, "Get in."

I felt safe enough to get in because she looked friendly and she then said, "I saw the strange man drive in this isolated area with you in the front seat, and I became suspicious and told my husband to follow him. Where do you live and what is your name?" I told her my name and that my father was at a friend's house, and I knew how to get there.

They drove me to the Jones' house and waited in the car. I got out of the car, went inside, and told the Jones' daughter I wanted to speak to my father. He was in the kitchen playing dominos with his friends. I grabbed him by the hand and said, "Daddy a lady wants to talk to you." without telling him why. He walked out the front door to the vehicle and the woman yelled at him, "You need to watch your daughter." I don't remember what else she said as I went into the house and sat on the sofa waiting for him to come back in. He came back in, didn't say a word to me, and went back into the kitchen to continue to play dominos. The Jones' daughter asked me questions about what happened, but I refused to answer. I sat there until almost dark waiting to go home. We started for home, neither of us spoke in the car nor when we arrived home.

Later that evening, there was a knock on the door. It was our ex-neighbor, and she had him with her. She was apologizing for him and said, "I know he scared you. The children will be so disappointed that you are not coming. Would you please come with us?" Daddy looked at me and said, "Doris do you want to go?" I said "No" with a voice I didn't know I had. It was with such finality. They left, and I never wanted to see them, or their children again and never have! That experience changed my life forever. I began to worry about my younger siblings but never told anyone about my concern. I took on the role of older sister and protector.

ADJUSTING

We were adjusting well to our new home and explored downtown Vallejo. There was a movie theatre called The Strain. It was nearly a three mile walk to downtown but we did it. The place we were not allowed to go was downtown lower Georgia Street which had record shops, bars, drunks and shootings. When I had money, I went to the record shop and bought an Aretha Franklin 45 record.

We never had money to go the movies. In our neighborhood there was a filling station that had soda machines on the outside and you could buy sodas by placing coins inside and receive bottles of cokes. The movies had a contest whereby if you found three coke bottle caps you could get into the movies for free. Every day I went down there looking on the ground for bottle caps. After a week of searching, I found enough bottle caps for me, Jeanette and Larry to go to The Strain and watch the movie **The Girl Can't Help It.** We stayed for two movies and walked home after dark.

After being in the house for a few years, Dee Dee, was talking about moving to Stockton to live with Aunt Nellie and attend the University of the Pacific. We continued to stay with Aunt Nellie during part of the summer. Trixie disappeared and we suspected he was picked up by the dog pound. It happened before when we lived in Chabot. We always got him out. We told my father and he said, "He was old anyway." We never saw Trixie again. Dee Dee attended Vallejo J.C. as well as Douglas and Charles. Dee Dee was smart, determined and disciplined. He was drafted into Army during the Korean War, after completing his duties, he returned and moved to Stockton and graduated from the university.

Larry, Doris, and Michael

Charles and Douglas also attended Vallejo J. C. and excelled in sports. Alma started dating a young man and shortly before her eighteenth 18, she told my father they wanted to get married. We knew his father as he was the only African American television repairman in the town. My father told her absolutely not, she was too young. Alma tried to rationalize with him by reminding him of how young my parents were when they married. I remember my father saying, "How do you know?" The arguing back and forth was intense. She cried, he yelled, etc. He eventually gave in and soon after her eighteenth birthday she got married. Aunt Nellie made her wedding dress. A year later, Virginia got married. We were told later, she was having a baby. Just like that they were both gone.

Aunt Bertie Mae and Uncle James got a divorce. This made us very sad. He moved to San Francisco where his daughter Betty lived, and Aunt Bertie found another husband, a younger man who was a minister. We continued to see her and attended his church. He got us, the younger kids, involved in the choir and we had to attend choir rehearsal often. He wanted me to lead a song in the children's choir one Sunday which I disliked very much. When it was time for me to sing, I decided right then and there in front of the church, I didn't want to sing. That man was so upset with me, I couldn't believe it. My siblings to this day still tease me about that.

The marriage did not last very long. She told us she was leaving California and moving to New York where she had a brother. We felt as if we were losing a mother. Uncle James also married again.

Alma's Wedding

GROWING UP

I started middle school at Franklin Junior High. It was very crowded and noisy in the hallways. Vallejo had two middle schools, Franklin and Vallejo Jr. My schedule allowed me to work in the office one period where my job was to deliver messages to the classrooms. We also got free lunch. I didn't like getting free lunch and felt embarrassed. I often skipped lunch. I delivered a message to the gym instructor and noticed the locker room was empty as the students were outside exercising. I don't know why, but I went through the lockers and took money that did not belong to me and used it to buy lunch. I continued to do it, knowing it was wrong. The thinking was they would have money the next day.

On occasion, I heard the women in the office where I worked, saying the students complained to the gym instructor their money was missing. Shortly after, they asked me to deliver a message to the gym instructor. Again, I went into the locker room, looked around and didn't see the instructor, and left being careful not to take anything. I returned to the office and told the secretary I couldn't deliver the message because there was no one there. Shortly after, I was no longer working in the office.

CLASSES

The required classes for us were home economics, business classes, art, etc. I very much liked the English, cooking and sewing courses. I got a job babysitting for my neighbor down the street who had two little boys named Chucky and Efrem as well as Winnie's five kids. I used the money to buy sewing materials and clothes. At the end of the semester, for our sewing class, we had to submit a completed project of a skirt, a blouse or a dress. I chose to make a skirt. I went to the fabric shop alone and chose a pattern and material for a skirt. The material I chose was a checkered black and brown one. My teacher told me it was going to be difficult to match up the checks. With the guidance of my teacher, I managed to finish the project and earned an A in the class. She asked me if I wanted to take part in the end of the semester fashion show wearing my skirt. I was too shy to do it. My father was very proud of the skirt I made.

My cooking instructor also asked me to serve at the ninth-grade graduation dinner. I was honored to do so. We all had to wear stockings, black skirts and white blouses. I walked the two miles to school to serve and walked home afterwards.

Doris Age 14

Doris, Rose, Nettie, Gloria

In addition to loving my classes, I loved hanging out with friends. My conversations were always with my friends, never with adults. My close friends were Rose and Gloria. We spent a lot of time listening to music in Gloria's garage and at Rose's house. While sitting on the school grounds, we discussed cutting a class. We decided to skip a class in the middle of the day. Rules were extremely strict then. You could not be late for a class, no talking in class, and students were constantly being sent to the principal's office if they disrupted the class. My friends and I thought they would not care because we were African Americans. We cut our last period class. The following morning, I was sitting in my English class when a student from the office came to the class and handed the teacher a note. She said, "Doris you are wanted in the principal's office. I was terrified. When I arrived, the principle said, "I know you cut class, and I know you did it with you friends. You girls always hang out together." I said, "I was sick." He said, "Bring a note from home saying you were sick." I turned red. The following morning, I caught my father just before he left for work and asked him to write me a note. "I missed my last period class because I was sick." He said, "Are you sure you were sick?"I knew he would be in a hurry to leave, and I said, "Yes I was sick." He wrote it and hurried out the door. I never cut again. I was too terrified. It was during this time our neighbors, an elderly Caucasian couple, nominated my father to be honored as father of the year. Daddy was smiling and said thank you.

For many years, my father suffered from ulcers. He seldom ate a meal. He had a friend who would cook dinner for us every evening Monday through Friday. She was a young, tall, large, African American woman by the name of Lorraine who lived within walking distance. She mostly fixed pots of food, often the same thing, but I loved her cooking. She was a nice woman who was living with her elderly mother. She taught me and Jeanette how to use the wringer washer we had. Jeanette would get her arm caught in the wringer and Lorraine would pop it open to release her arm. I can still see Jeanette's arm going through the wringer.

My father had been a smoker most of his life. He started smoking as a teenager in the back woods of Shreveport. His choice of cigarettes was Pall Mall and Camels, and he would often roll his own. He was not a chain smoker as I doubt, he could have afforded to smoke all day long. One evening, I heard him fall on the floor and moan in pain. I went into his room and asked him what was wrong. He could not speak. I called the operator and told her of my father's condition and asked for an ambulance. A few minutes later, she called back and said you forgot to give me your address. The ambulance arrived, took him to Kaiser Hospital where he was diagnosed as having bleeding ulcers. He had surgery and was in the hospital for over a week.

HIGH SCHOOL

After graduating from junior high, I went on to Vallejo Senior High. There were so many students as we were the baby-boomers. During the 11th Grade we were split into two sessions. The following semester, it was decided that some of us would have to be transferred to Hogan High School. The students that had to transfer cried. Some of them I never saw again. I continued to take business courses including typing, shorthand, filing and bookkeeping. We learned to type on a blank typewriter. Our instructor wrote the letters and numbers on the blackboard correlating with the keyboard rows. She would say the letters or numbers and we would type them, handing in our papers at the end of class.

I was very thin, and I wanted to save my money, so I would only eat a twenty-five-cent grilled cheese sandwich in order to save for clothes, hair appointments, and makeup. I would babysit Virginia and Alma's kids and my Cousin Winnie's five kids too.

Dee Dee, Douglas and Charles were dating and introduced their girlfriends to us, Marcia, Helen and Joanne. We were excited to meet them. Marcia and Helen were from Stockton and Joanne from Vallejo.

FRIDAY NOVEMBER 22, 1963

It was a sunny, cool morning, so just an ordinary day. I attended my last morning class, which was my typing class, and proceeded to my locker right outside of my class to put my books away. A boy had a locker next to me, said in a very fast tone, "the President has been shot." I said what? He repeated it. I just looked at him and said, "I don't believe it."

Just then the door to my typing class flew open and the teacher came out with a shocked look on her face.

I went to the cafeteria, and everyone was saying the same thing, "the President has been shot!" Classes were dismissed, the school buses were lining up, and we got on the bus for home.

We were glued to the television watching Walter Cronkite updating the nation on the President's condition. My father returned home early from work and told all of us to watch television and remember what we saw and heard.

My sister Carolyn was so upset; she was put on a bus early to come home from work and cried the entire evening. My father could not comfort her. To this day she does not like to talk about it.

We never left the house the entire weekend. We only watched the updates and funeral.

GRADUATION, 1964

Practicing with our caps and gowns and Graduation were exciting. Some of the high achieving girls had already landed secretarial jobs at Mare Island, insurance companies and the State of California offices. Others went on to college. The graduating class was one of the largest in Vallejo High School's history. We were the baby boomers.

I continued my education by going on to Vallejo J.C. as did most of my friends. I always had a problem with transportation. One of my high school friends Barbara, a Chinese student, lived near to me, and her father had purchased a car for her. I asked her for a ride home and she said, "Sure, but I have to let you out a few blocks away because I don't want my father to find out I had passengers." We continued this arrangement, and Barbara would pick me up in the morning. I would duck down in the seat as she passed her parents' home. We did this for approximately a year until her father caught us.

I started taking the city bus that took an hour to get to school. On occasion, my father would drive me to school, using my brother, Howard's, red Impala. Howard had been drafted into the Army and was serving in Vietnam.

After graduation, I continued to date my high school boyfriend. He was now attending Merritt College in Oakland, taking courses to become a doctor. He was drafted into the Army; we married, and he was deployed to Vietnam two months later.

I decided to seek employment and took a Greyhound bus to San Francisco to the business district which had many employment service agencies. I walked into a publishing firm. I was given a skills test that I passed. I was told thank you for coming and that was it. I continued walking and went into a law firm applying for a position as a legal secretary. I was interviewed and waited for a response. A young African American man flirted with me and said, I would hire you. I never heard back. I took the bus back home. The following day I went back to the bus stop and asked where I could catch a bus in San Francisco for the Hunters Point Shipyard. I was given instructions and left for San Francisco. I went to the Human Resources Department of the Shipyard and was interviewed by June Dickoff. She said we have a position here in Human Resources, and she was impressed that I had an AA Degree and was married to a person in the military. I accepted the job, and she said, "But you have to live in San Francisco." I said, "I will be moving in with my aunt and uncle who live in San Francisco". Now I had to make good on my word as I had not told my uncle or my father.

45

I called Uncle James and told him I had accepted a position at the Navy yard and asked if I could move in with him and Aunt Odessa. He said he needed to talk to Odessa and he would let me know. He called me back and said yes.

I then told my father and asked him how much I should give Uncle James for rent? He said talk to him. I did and we worked it out. I told him I would return home on the weekends.

Uncle James was an intelligent, uneducated, and hard-working man who painted houses in San Francisco. He had two adult children from his first marriage, and we always considered them intelligent. His daughter, Betty, worked at the shipyard and his son, James Ray, was in the Navy and had become a speech writer for a colonel. Uncle James only painted occasionally now, as he developed problems with his arches from standing on ladders. Odessa worked in the hospital and was a breast cancer survivor. She showed me the prosthesis she wore. I had never heard of women getting breast cancer until she told me about it.

The shipyard was a mile from his home. I would walk to the bus stop at 6:30 am catch the bus which passed by a pig slaughterhouse three blocks from the shipyard. In the mornings you could not smell it, but every evening after getting off at 4pm the smell was so bad I always had to cover my nose. My uncle's neighbor worked at the slaughterhouse and always generously gave my uncle pig's feet. Odessa would make hog head cheese, something I never had before, and I loved it.

My first day on the job, Mrs. Kickoff introduced me to a young, somewhat overweight African American woman by the name of Jenny. She said, "Do you know how blessed you are to be hired here in Human Resources? I didn't know why she said that. "I want to show you around the shipyard. We started with the steno pool.

We walked to several building then the building that housed the steno pool. I saw rows and rows of typists. They were all African American women. I understood what she meant. The racism it implied.

Everything became routine. I went to work, took the bus home on the weekends and returned to San Francisco. On occasion, Jeanette would take the bus to San Francisco, and we both went shopping downtown. I loved the town, my job and co-workers.

Aunt Bertie Mae and I communicated via letter for many years. When I moved to San Francisco I told her I was now living with Uncle James. She wrote back wishing me well. I now had her letters coming to my uncle's home. I told him I stayed in contact with her. She had gotten married again to a Puerto Rican man by the last name of Molina. To my surprise, he said, "She is not your aunt anymore." I had no idea there was such animosity between them. She never spoke badly of him.

James and Odessa Grant

I started going to church with them and getting my hair done at Odessa's hairdresser. Odessa had a daughter that lived in another state, and she seldom spoke of her. I could tell the relationship was not close. I met my cousin Betty for lunch at the shipyard, and she said, "Girl, Ronnie came to my house dressed in women's clothing." I just looked at her in amazement, not knowing what to say. I was aware Ronnie was now living in San Francisco, but he had not seen us or talked to us for several years.

Aunt Bertie Mae called me at Uncle James one evening, and he answered the phone. He spoke to her for a few minutes then put me on the phone. I was pleased and surprised. He seemed to change towards me and said she stole some money from him. Years later, I asked her about that, and she said she never took anything from him that did not belong to her. I believe her. My relationship with my uncle seemed to change. He was cold towards me. Odessa became closer to me.

I stayed home from work due to a cold. My job called the house. It was Janet, my supervisor asking me where a certain file was. My aunt said they were checking to see if I was truthful about living in San Francisco. Approximately a year later, there were rumors the government would be closing some shipyards and Hunters Point was on the list to be closed. Many employees asked me about how it was living in Vallejo as some would be transferred to Mare Island. I felt as if I was again coming between my uncle and Aunt Bertie as I remembered as a child. I told them I was moving back to Vallejo to live with my father. My uncle said fine. Odessa was sad and she drove me to the bus station, gave me a hug and I returned home to live with my father. I commuted via Greyhound bus, not telling my supervisor. It was very hard as I left home at 5:30 am, walked to the corner on Sonoma Blvd and caught a bus to downtown San Francisco, transferred and caught another bus to Hunters Point. If you were more than fifteen minutes late, you were charged with one day of vacation time. I managed to get in a carpool and commuted with three guys who also worked at the shipyard. There was never any mention of them living in Vallejo. I felt uncomfortable riding with them, as they constantly flirted with me. I put an ad in the paper that I was looking to commute to San Francisco. A white guy that drove a sports car answered the ad and I commuted with him. He was a nice guy and a gentleman. He always offered to drive me to my doorstep. I never wanted him to see where I lived. One evening, he insisted. My father was standing on the porch and watched as I got out of his car. Before I could get in the house he said, "So you are commuting with a white man?" I didn't say a word, just went into the house. My father had problems with white men due to the racism he had experienced while growing up in Louisiana. I stopped commuting with him and quit my job to seek employment in Vallejo.

Virginia was now living with my father as she was separated from her husband and had three young children. She was distraught, stressed and cried to my father, "What am I going to do with my life with three kids, where can I go?" My father said, "Don't worry, you are staying here, we will work it out."

Christmas card to Douglas Grant from Bertie Mae

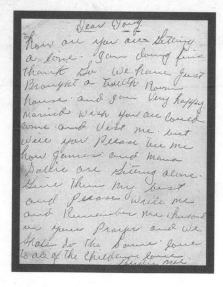

Postcard to Douglas Grant from Bertie Mae and husband Molina

She was very helpful and gave me advice about my English and manner of dress. I applied for a secretarial position at the Bank of America in downtown Vallejo. There were four of us waiting to be interviewed; three white girls I was second from the left. Just then, a young white man tapped me on my shoulder and said, "The hiring manager will not have time to interview you. I will give you a short interview." When I returned home, my father asked me if they had interviewed me. I told him the manager said he did not have time. I never heard back.

Slick, Aunt Nellie, Daddy

I eventually was hired at EEOP as a secretary to the Director of the Head start Program for Solano County. The job was within walking distance from my father's home. My husband called me and said he wanted me to meet him in Hawaii. I packed my bags but was afraid to get on the plane. My supervisor was a hippy who drove a Volkswagen van, was married with three children and had marital problems. I always felt he was jealous of my status as I had no children and so much freedom.

My husband bought me a canary yellow hatch back Mustang with black leather seats which I couldn't drive. He taught me as much as he could, and my brother Larry also taught me how to drive. While driving, I ran into a concrete wall and tore up the front bumper. I went to a repair shop, got it fixed, and threw the old bumper into the trunk.

MARRIED LIFE AFTER VIETNAM

When I returned home one evening, there was a knock on the door. My father answered and there was a young man in a uniform asking to speak to me. My father said, "Doris go to the living room and let me talk to him". I went back in the living room wondering what was going on. My father said Doris come to the door. It was someone from the Red Cross saying my husband had been injured in Vietnam and transported to a hospital in Japan. I called him in Japan. Subsequently he was transferred to the Presidio in San Francisco to recover from his leg injuries. I went to visit him and noticed how thin and depressed he looked. He had a faraway look on his face.

He was released and eventually we rented a two-bedroom duplex in Vallejo and started a family.

I introduced him to my coworkers. The assistant director of EEOC, Steve was a car fanatic. He had my husband show him the car and they opened the trunk and discovered the bent front bumper. They both looked at me and laughed. I then had to explain how it got there. I never forgot that moment.

We decided to visit my Aunt Bertie in New York. We were excited as neither of us had ever been to New York. I had my sister Virginia keep the kids for me and off we went. We met her husband Molina (his last name) and got along quite well with him. He especially took to my husband. Aunt Bertie wished I had brought the children with me as she loved children.

Aunt Sallie was now living with Uncle James and Odessa in San Francisco. Her eye sight was failing but her memory was still sharp. She recognized me by my voice when I last saw her. After her death in October 1971, at the age of 96, Odessa gave me Aunt Sallie's bible in which Aunt Sallie had noted her birth date, November 8, 1875, as well as birth dates, and marriages of her siblings, children, and parents, a common way to keep family records.

We stayed for a week visiting the landmarks in Manhattan, and took a bus to Washington DC, visiting the white house, and the Smithsonian. I visited her second time with my sisters Jeanette and Alma.

Two years later, I had a strange premonition, a nightmare, a dream, I don't know. I had a headache and fell asleep on the sofa. I suddenly heard the front door open. My first thought was "Did I forget to lock the front door?" A man entered wearing a black suit that was hanging on his thin body. He walked with a purpose, and his eyes were as bright as two head lights. I stayed still hoping he would not see me. Suddenly he turned and looked at me. I screamed, but I could not hear myself scream. I heard a woman's voice say, "Should we take her?" I screamed even louder. He said, "No!" He walked up to me and placed his hand on my stomach. He had one long middle finger. After he did that, I became suddenly calm. I saw myself rising to the ceiling looking down at my body that appeared old. Just then, I sat straight up. The room was quiet and dark. I ran into the bedroom and kept the light on until my husband returned home. I told him about the vision.

1977, THE MURDER

On occasion, my father would complain about his leg hurting, and frequently it was when he was in bed. I put it out of my mind. He continued to visit his friend, Mr. Hicks, at his home where they would play dominoes, and he would return home at night. Mr. Hicks was a longtime friend who came to our home while we were still in high school, and the two would play card games. Mr. Hick's wife had become too ill for him to care for, and he had had to place her in a care facility.

I stopped by my father's house on my lunch hour one day and noticed a card on his door from the Vallejo Police Department. Not knowing why, I called my sister Alma and told her about it. She said Mr. Hicks had been murdered, and the police wanted to talk to my father. Total shock!

I saw my father later that day, and he was very nervous. When he spoke to the police, my father told them that Mr. Hicks had had a young Black male renting a room at his home, but his wife did not like him, so the renter was asked to move out. The young man was suspected of returning to Mr. Hicks' home after my father left for the day and bludgeoned him to death. The young man was arrested and charged.

My sister, Virginia, called me a few weeks later and said my father had become ill and had fallen in Lucky's grocery store. The manager called my brother Charles after calling an ambulance. He was diagnosed as having had a stroke. I found that hard to believe. After many tests were given, and our complaining that we felt there was something else wrong with him, Kaiser finally ran a test and discovered my father had cancer that had spread to his brain. It took me back to 1955. I just never thought he would become ill. He never complained about an illness. We had a new doctor put on his case, and he had brain surgery to remove the growth. It could have originated in the lungs. He was in and out of the hospital. Larry planned a family dinner for him to be held on his birthday in March at the Elegant Farmer Restaurant, Jack London Square in Oakland. We all attended. He thanked us but he didn't eat anything.

May 1978, He seemed to be doing better. He was smiling whenever we went to see him. Alma called me on a Saturday and said, "Doris we must go visit Daddy today". I said, "Go ahead. I am not ready yet, and I will take my own car". I continued to clean up, and after a few hours I started to get dressed when she called me again and told me not to come because he passed away peacefully. I wanted to see him, and I started to cry. Alma was as calm as I had seen her since his illness began. Before, she had always been so worried and nervous. She said she had taken her seven-year-old son, Eric, with her, but kids were not allowed in the room, so she told my father she would be right back. When she returned to his room, he looked at her for a few minutes, closed his eyes and died.

After his death, many family members and friends asked "How did he do it? How did we manage to stay together and become successful, get an education, and never have a criminal record?"

WHY?

In 2011, my niece wanted all of us to gather at a studio in Sacramento for a group picture. It was not easy trying to get us all together. A week after taking the picture, she told us our picture was going to appear in the Vallejo Times Herald newspaper along with a story about us. We were all surprised.

My nephew said, "Aunt Doris, there should be something written about your family. I found notes I have and said, "Could it be? Should there be?" I'm not a writer, but I decided to turn my notes into a story some might want to read. A friend who had already written a book about her family encouraged me.

Grant Family Article Page 1

Grant Family Article Page 2

Grant Family Portrait 2011

Doris 1995

Virginia, Alma, Carolyn, Doris, Jeanette 1992

Doris, Around 1994

My brothers, Charles and Douglas Jr. attended Sacramento State University on sports scholarships. Douglas moved in with Uncle J.P. During high school he received many sports accommodations being a basketball player whose team finished second in the State in 1956-57. He was inducted in Vallejo Sports Hall of Fame. Both boys ran track in high school and at Sacramento State. Douglas' coach at Sacramento State got him a room over a mortuary in which to stay, and he allowed Charles to stay there secretly.

Douglas left college and became employed by the State of California, Sacramento Department of EDD and retired after 40 plus years of service. He joined the National Guard and remained in it for over twenty years. He married Helen and had a son and a daughter and raised a granddaughter.

Charles graduated from Sacramento State University with a degree in criminal justice. He married Joanne and had five children. He worked at the Vacaville prison facility, became one of the best probation officers in Alameda and Contra Costa Counties.

Archy completed his master's degree in criminal justice at the University of California at Davis and became a supervisor at Folsom Youth Authority. He married Marcia and had two children and a third child by his second wife.

Virginia divorced and moved to Sacramento where she raised her five children. She went back to school and graduated with a degree in child development. She worked as a preschool teacher with the Sacramento Public School District for 25 plus years.

Alma married right after high school at the age eighteen. She moved to Sacramento where she worked for many years as the secretary for a prominent, well-known, African -American attorney. She had three children and obtained a law degree at JFK University in Sacramento.

Howard returned home safely from Vietnam, but he only stayed home a short while. There was constant tension between him and our father. After one of their many arguments, Howard moved to Sonoma, finished his education at Sonoma State and became employed at Sonoma State Hospital. He married and had two children. Years later, he was nominated as "father of the year".

Carolyn married and had twin girls and a younger daughter. She always worked and never seemed to be interested in furthering her education. She worked at an elementary school and at Mare Island. She was shy, quiet and stayed around her family. When the shipyard closed, she was offered a transfer to the shipyard in San Diego. She decided not to take that job. After her children grew up, she attended San Francisco State, and graduated with a master's degree in counseling. Later in life she became a counselor at Vacaville prison where she counseled prisoners who were returning to civilian life.

I took various evening classes as I always had a job during the day and was taking care of two children. I worked at Solano County, Sacramento City College and obtained a divorce. I made the decision to pursue a degree. I accepted a position at Peralta Colleges in Oakland worked at campus police and human resources obtained a Bachelor of Science degree in business management and taught as a part-time instructor. Later, I obtained a real estate license. I retired after working for forty plus years and married again years later.

Jeanette and Michael were the only two still living with my father. After the home we had lived in for so many years was condemned and torn down, our father bought another home in Vallejo. However, he kept the land from the first one.

Jeanette was always a very hard-working student who earned good grades. She left home and rented the downstairs apartment from some friends in Oakland for a while. She and Larry got an apartment together in Oakland while pursuing her studies at Golden Gate University, San Francisco; she earned a degree in Legal Science. She attended Hayward State, where she obtained a masters degree in Public Administration. She became friends with Betty Gatlin who was the choir director at Allen Temple Baptist Church of Oakland. Jeanette sang in the choir and eventually became the president of the choir. She invited me to attend and I later joined Allen Temple, was baptized and became an active member, Jeanette retired after working at UC Berkeley as benefits coordinator. It was there our cousin Wilbur was working at Lawrence Lab, came to the benefits office, and saw Jeanette not knowing she worked there. We stay in contact with him.

Larry left home and moved to Sacramento, where he lived for a while with Uncle J.P. He attended Sacramento State and was involved with acting and was cast in several plays. He obtained a bachelor's degree in Criminal Justice from Sacramento State, married and had two children. Later Larry and his son both graduated from college at the same time, and this time Larry obtained a law degree, his son a bachelors degree. He married a second time.

Michael, he found employment at the Sacramento Municipal Utility District (SMUD) where he, like my father, never took a day off or time off for a vacation.

House Being Demolished 1979

Disadvantaged families in this world can and do become productive citizens. I am alarmed by the amount of violence committed against African Americans and by those within the race. Having a purpose in life, examples, a dream, drive, and determination are what it takes to be successful. Staying out of trouble at a young age seems harder now than ever. Remembering one mistake made as a young person will and does haunt and follow you for the rest of your life. At times it will even cost you an opportunity to fulfill your dreams. Talking to each other and learning something about each other's lives, culture and customs is the key. My common ground with others is food. I enjoy all types of food, and I am always open minded about trying something new.

One thing, eight of the eleven of us suffer from diabetes. Could it have been stress, genetics or a combination of both? The jury is still out.

As life has it, you lose relatives and friends along the way:

Isadore Andrews died in 1971

Aunt Nellie died in 1976

Aunt Bertie Mae died of a heart attack in 1976

Ronnie died from complications of AIDS 1986

Vicky while walking across a street in Stockton was hit by a speeding driver and passed away in 1979

Uncle James died in 1982 Aunt Odessa moved to Houston and passed away years later

Betty and James Ray died a week apart in 1985, Betty of lung cancer, James Ray of a heart attack.

Cousin Winnie died, 2018

As for the rest of us: as of the writing of this, <u>Douglas Jr, Virginia and Michael passed away between 2018-2019</u>

We currently have children, and cousins that are NFL and CBS sports newscasters and directors, a veterinarian, respiratory therapist, court reporter, minister, business owners, professional singers, law enforcement officers, just to name a few.

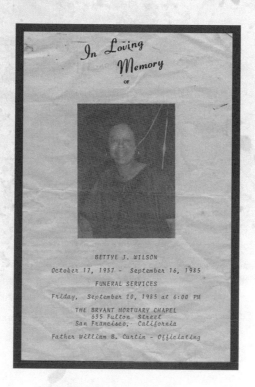

In Loving Memory

OF

BETTYE J. WILSON

October 17, 1937 - September 16, 1985

FUNERAL SERVICES

Friday, September 20, 1985 at 6:00 PM

THE BRYANT MORTUARY CHAPEL
635 Fulton Street
San Francisco, California

Father William B. Curtin - Officiating

Betty Grant Wilson (Victoria)

Printed in the United States
by Baker & Taylor Publisher Services